AF416293

Navigating the Emotional Storm: The Ultimate Guide to Understanding, Dealing with, and Transforming Anger

From Recognizing the Signs to Effective Communication: Strategies, Exercises, and Testimonials for a Life Free from Anger Explosions and Renewed Emotional Well-being

Giacomo Salvati

Introduction: Anger and Its Place in Our Lives Anger is one of the fundamental emotions of human beings, alongside joy, sadness, fear, and love. Throughout various stages of life, all of us experience moments of anger. Whether it's a traffic mishap, a dispute with a colleague, or deep personal frustration, anger has the capacity to emerge at the most unexpected times. But why is anger so important? Why can't we simply ignore or suppress it? Anger, like every emotion, serves a purpose. It can signal to us that something is amiss, that one of our rights has been violated, or that our expectations have not been met. It is an alarm bell telling us to pay attention, to defend our needs, or to seek a change. However, when not managed correctly, anger can transform into a silent enemy that erodes our well-being, our relationships, and our quality of life.

The importance of managing anger extends beyond preventing unpleasant episodes or emotional outbursts. It involves understanding oneself, building healthy relationships, and living a balanced and fulfilling life. Unmanaged anger can lead to health problems such as hypertension and heart disease, damage personal and professional relationships, and diminish our ability to savor life's small joys.

In this book, we will embark on a journey to understand the nature of anger, its causes, and how it can be effectively and constructively managed. Through examples, real-life stories, strategies, and techniques, I hope to provide you with the tools necessary to address anger in a healthy way and transform it into a positive force in your life.

Managing anger does not mean eliminating this emotion, but rather learning how to express anger appropriately, how to listen to its message, and how to use it as a compass to steer our actions in a positive direction. I invite you to join me on this path of discovery, awareness, and transformation.

Chapter 1: Introduction to Anger

Anger: A Definition Anger is an intense emotion that all of us have experienced at least once in our lives. It manifests as a reaction to a perceived threat or injustice, whether real or imagined, and can vary in intensity from mild annoyance to deep fury. It is a natural response and, in certain contexts, can even be considered protective or adaptive.

But before delving into why we get angry, let's precisely define what "anger" means. Anger can be defined as an intense emotional reaction that occurs in response to an event or situation perceived as threatening or frustrating. It can manifest through various behaviors, thoughts, and physical sensations, such as flushing of the face, an increased heart rate, or a desire to react physically or verbally.

Biological and Psychological Origins of Anger

Biological Aspects: Like many other animals, humans have developed defense mechanisms to cope with potentially dangerous situations. These mechanisms are rooted in our biology. When you perceive a threat, your body responds by releasing a series of hormones, including adrenaline and cortisol. These hormones prepare the body for an immediate response, often described as "fight or flight." It is an evolutionary heritage that allowed us to survive in hostile environments. In response to these hormonal secretions, the heart rate may increase, muscles may tense, and attention may focus on the source of the threat. This is the biology of anger in action.

Psychological Aspects: From a psychological perspective, anger often arises from perceptions, thoughts, or beliefs related to injustice, violation of one's rights, or the inability to achieve a goal. This is why two people can react differently to the same situation: it depends on how they interpret and evaluate that situation. Some of us are more prone to anger due to past life experiences, trauma, or learned patterns during childhood. For example, if you learned as a child that expressing anger is the only way to get attention or to defend your rights, you may carry this behavioral pattern into adulthood.

In conclusion, anger is a complex interplay between biology and psychology. Understanding both of these aspects helps us recognize anger when it arises and develop strategies to manage it in a healthy and constructive manner. As we continue on our journey, we will further explore how these two dimensions influence each other and how we can work on them to improve our relationship with anger.

Chapter 2: The Importance of Anger Management

Consequences of Anger on Health: Not Just an Emotional Issue When we think of anger, we tend to focus on its immediate manifestations: shouting, heated arguments, and, in some cases, aggressive behaviors. However, the scope of anger's repercussions goes far beyond its visible manifestations. Chronic or unmanaged anger can have profound implications for our physical and mental health.

Physical Health and Anger: A Troubling Connection

1. Cardiovascular Issues: Frequent or intense anger can increase the risk of heart disease. The increased heart rate and blood pressure, typical responses to anger, can, over the long term, damage blood vessels and the heart.
2. Compromised Immune System: Repeated episodes of anger can weaken the immune

system, making the body more vulnerable to infections and illnesses.
3. Digestive Problems: Anger can interfere with digestion, leading to symptoms such as gastritis or ulcers.
4. Insomnia: The tension and stress associated with anger can affect the quality of sleep.

Mental Health: The Hidden Shadow of Anger

1. Anxiety and Depression: Chronic anger can lead to prolonged periods of anxiety. If left unmanaged, anger can also lead to feelings of helplessness, which are linked to depression.
2. Reduced Quality of Relationships: Uncontrolled anger can damage relationships with friends, family, and colleagues, leading to feelings of isolation and loneliness.
3. Low Self-Esteem: Living in a state of constant irritation or frustration can negatively impact self-perception and self-esteem.

4. Substance Abuse: Some individuals may use alcohol or drugs as a means to manage or suppress anger, which can lead to addiction and further mental health issues.

In Conclusion: Anger Beyond the Momentary Outburst Managing anger is not just about avoiding conflicts or episodes of rage; it's about protecting our overall well-being. Uncontrolled anger comes at a high cost, both physically and mentally. Recognizing the importance of managing anger and taking active steps toward effective management is the first step toward a healthier and more balanced life. Throughout this book, we will further explore how to do this, providing tools and strategies for healthy anger management. Chapter 3: Recognizing Early Signs

Awareness Before the Explosion: The Importance of Recognizing Signs One fundamental aspect of anger management is the ability to recognize early signs before anger takes over. These signs can manifest both physically and emotionally. Being aware of them allows us to intervene before the situation escalates, making anger management easier and more effective.

Identifying Body Signals: The Physiology of Anger

1. Increased Heart Rate: One of the first signs of impending anger can be a rapid or pounding heartbeat.
2. Muscle Tension: You may feel tension, especially in the shoulders, jaw, or fists.
3. Shallow Breathing: Breathing may become shallower and faster.
4. Sweating: Some people may start to sweat, especially on their hands or forehead.
5. Sensations of Heat or Cold: You might experience waves of heat or, conversely, shivers.
6. Upset Stomach: Anger can also manifest as a feeling of discomfort or nausea.

Emotional Signs of Approaching Anger: Reading Emotions

1. Irritability: This is often the initial sign. Small things that would normally roll off your back can start to irritate you.
2. Frustration: Feeling helpless or stuck in a situation can be a precursor to anger.
3. Sense of Injustice: The perception that something is not fair or that your rights have been violated.
4. Anxiety or Panic Feelings: Increasing tension can manifest as anxiety.
5. Desire to React: A strong inner urge to respond, which can manifest as a desire to yell, throw something, or even react physically.

In Conclusion: Prevent Rather Than Cure
The old adage "prevention is better than cure" is particularly true when it comes to anger. Recognizing these early signs gives you a window of opportunity to intervene, take a moment to calm down, and assess the situation rationally. In the upcoming chapters, we will learn various techniques and strategies to do just that, addressing anger proactively rather than reactively.
Chapter 4: Origins of Anger

Roots of Anger: Seeking the Deep Causes
Anger, like all emotions, doesn't arise out of nowhere. It has roots that can be traced to various experiences, situations, or internal feelings. Understanding where anger comes from can help not only manage it better but also prevent or reduce it. Let's explore some common causes.

Daily Stress and Frustrations: Continuous Tension

1. Pressures of Modern Life: We live in a fast-paced world with many demands and expectations weighing on us. These pressures can accumulate, creating a state of chronic stress that makes it easier to slip into anger.
2. Obstacles and Unexpected Hurdles: When our plans are disrupted or we encounter unexpected obstacles, frustration can quickly build.
3. Relational Conflicts: Disagreements with partners, family, friends, or colleagues can easily fuel feelings of anger.
4. Workplace Issues: Challenges such as excessive workloads, conflicts with coworkers, or job dissatisfaction can be significant sources of stress and anger.

Past Traumatic or Negative Experiences: The Shadow of the Past

1. Abuse or Violence: Individuals who have experienced physical, emotional, or sexual

abuse may carry deep-seated repressed anger.

2. Loss and Grief: The loss of a loved one, a relationship, or an opportunity can trigger feelings of anger, especially if the loss is perceived as unjust.
3. Childhood Experiences: Events or circumstances during childhood, such as being a victim of bullying, neglect, or growing up in an unstable family environment, can leave emotional scars that manifest as anger in adulthood.
4. Accumulated Trauma: Sometimes, it's not a single traumatic event but a series of small traumas or injustices accumulated over time that fuel anger.

In Conclusion: Introspection and Understanding The origins of anger can be complex and interconnected. Taking the time to reflect on the deep causes of your feelings of anger can offer valuable insights on how to manage it. With understanding, we can develop empathy for ourselves and targeted strategies to address triggering situations and emotions. In the following chapters, we will further explore these aspects, providing tools and techniques to address the roots of our anger.

Chapter 5: The Different Types of Anger

Shades of Anger: Beyond Just Being "Mad" Anger is not a monolithic emotion. It has various shades and intensities, and understanding the different types of anger can help us manage it more effectively. Each form of anger has its unique manifestations, causes, and potential solutions.

1. Passive Anger: Definition: This is a subtle form of anger that isn't openly expressed. The person may avoid conflicts but expresses their anger through passive-aggressive behaviors. Manifestations: Sarcasm, chronic lateness, hostile behavior in the form of "jokes" or caustic comments.

2. Explosive Anger: Definition: This form of anger is sudden and intense, often in response to provocation. It can manifest as an outburst of fury. Manifestations: Yelling, breaking objects, physical aggression.

3. Repressed Anger: Definition: Repressed anger is when feelings of anger are held inside and not expressed, accumulating over time. Manifestations: Chronic tension, irritability, a feeling of being "on the verge," health problems like headaches or hypertension.

4. Resentful Anger: Definition: Arising from a sense of injustice or unresolved old wounds and grudges. Manifestations: Dwelling on past wrongs, difficulty forgiving, vengeful behavior.

5. Constructive Anger: Definition: This form of anger is used as a catalyst for positive change. It's a controlled state of anger directed toward problem resolution. Manifestations: Advocacy, fighting for justice, involvement in social causes.

6. Chronic Anger: Definition: It's a persistent state of irritability that may not be tied to a specific cause. People with chronic anger are often angry much of the time. Manifestations: Constant irritability, pessimism, a tendency to see the worst in situations.

In Conclusion: Personalizing Anger Management Identifying the specific type of anger you are experiencing can provide valuable insights into how to address it. Not all strategies work for every type of anger, so understanding your own shade of anger can help you choose the most effective approach. In the upcoming chapters, we will provide tools and techniques that can be customized based on the type of anger you are dealing with.

Chapter 6: Emotional Self-Awareness

At the Heart of Emotions: The Art of Knowing Oneself Emotional self-awareness is not just the ability to recognize when you are angry but also to understand why and how emotions interact with each other. This chapter will explore how to learn to listen to and interpret your own emotions, providing exercises to develop greater awareness.

Exploring Your Emotions: The Inner Journey

1. The Language of Emotions: Each emotion has a message. For example, anger may indicate that you've experienced an injustice, while sadness may suggest a loss.
2. Emotional Interconnectedness: We rarely feel just one emotion at a time. Anger might be accompanied by disappointment, pain, or shame.
3. Nonjudgmental Listening: Exploring emotions without judgment allows you to truly understand where they come from.

Exercises to Develop Awareness: Daily Practices

1. Emotion Journal: Dedicate a few minutes each day to write down how you feel. This can help you recognize recurring patterns or triggers.
2. Meditation: The practice of meditation can help you become more aware of your emotions and thoughts, offering a moment of introspection.
3. Emotional Check-Ins: During the day, pause for a moment and ask yourself, "How am I feeling right now?" This can help you develop the habit of recognizing and naming your emotions.
4. Self-Dialogue: When you feel particularly emotional, try asking yourself a question like, "Why do I feel this way?" or "What triggered this emotion?"
5. Art and Creativity: Expressing yourself through art, writing, or music can be a powerful way to explore and understand your emotions.

In Conclusion: Awareness as a Compass Emotional self-awareness is like an internal compass. When we truly understand our emotions, we can navigate life with greater intention and purpose. By developing a deeper relationship with your emotions, you are better equipped to address, manage, and transform anger constructively. In the following chapters, we will explore specific tools and strategies for anger management built on this fundamental emotional awareness.

Chapter 7: Breathing and Relaxation Techniques

Breathing with Purpose: The Key to a Calm Heart The power of breath in anger management cannot be underestimated. The simple act of conscious breathing can act as a switch, transforming a moment of intense anger into a pause for reflection. This chapter will introduce various breathing and relaxation techniques, complete with practical exercises.

The Connection Between Breath and Anger When we're angry, our breathing becomes faster and shallower, and our bodies prepare for action. Taking control of our breathing can help return the body to a state of calm, creating space to react with greater clarity and awareness.

Breathing Exercises

1. Deep Breathing:
   - Sit or lie down in a comfortable position.
   - Inhale slowly through your nose, feeling your diaphragm and stomach expand.
   - Hold for a brief pause.
   - Exhale slowly through your mouth, releasing all the air.
   - Repeat for 3-5 minutes.
2. Breath Counting:
   - Inhale slowly, counting to four.
   - Hold your breath for a count of four.
   - Exhale slowly, counting to four.
   - Repeat for 3-5 minutes.
3. Belly Breathing:
   - Place one hand on your chest and the other on your stomach.
   - Inhale deeply from your diaphragm, feeling only your stomach rise.
   - Exhale slowly, feeling your stomach fall.
   - Repeat for 3-5 minutes.

Relaxation Techniques

1. Progressive Muscle Relaxation:
    - Start from your feet and work your way up to your head, tensing and then releasing each muscle group for 5-10 seconds.
    - Focus on the feeling of relaxation that follows tension.
2. Positive Visualization:
    - Close your eyes and imagine a place or situation that makes you feel calm and happy.
    - Immerse yourself in this imagery, noting the colors, sounds, and sensations.
3. Mindful Listening:
    - Play relaxing music or nature sounds.
    - Focus on the sound, bringing your attention back whenever your mind wanders.

In Conclusion: One Breath at a Time In moments of intense anger, breathing and relaxation techniques can be your most powerful allies. By practicing regularly, they become tools you can use automatically when faced with stressful situations. In the next chapter, we will delve into effective communication, building on the foundation of calm and clarity created through these techniques.

Chapter 8: Effective Communication

Speaking from the Heart: The Art of Nonviolent Communication Effective communication goes beyond the words we choose; it also involves tone, body language, and intention. When it comes to expressing anger or frustration, the ability to communicate non-aggressively becomes crucial. This chapter explores how to express your emotions constructively and respectfully, protecting relationships and fostering mutual understanding.

Anger and Communication Expressed aggressively or passively, anger can erode trust and damage relationships. However, when channeled through effective communication, anger can become a catalyst for change and growth.

Principles of Nonviolent Communication

1. Nonjudgmental Observation: Avoid labeling or judging. Simply express what you have observed.
2. Express Feelings: Communicate how you feel about what you have observed without assigning blame.
3. Express Needs: Share the needs or desires underlying your feelings.
4. Make Clear Requests: Indicate what you would like to happen in a clear and positive manner.

Strategies for Effective Communication

1. Active Listening: Fully focus on the other person when they speak, avoiding interruptions or formulating mental responses.
2. "I" Instead of "You": Begin sentences with "I feel" or "I think" instead of pointing fingers with "You always" or "You never."

3. Seek Clarification: If you're unsure you've understood, ask the other person to repeat or explain further.
4. Avoid Escalation: If the conversation becomes too tense, take a break and return when both parties are calmer.
5. Practice Empathy: Try to put yourself in the other person's shoes, seeking to understand their feelings and perspectives.

Exercises for Effective Communication
1. Role-Play: Practice with a friend or family member, taking on the role of expressing a concern and the role of listening, and then switch roles.
2. Journaling: Write down a situation in which you felt angry, then rewrite it expressing your feelings and needs constructively.
3. Feedback: After a discussion with someone, ask for feedback on how you communicated. This can help you identify areas for improvement.

In Conclusion: Words as Bridges Words have the power to build bridges or create barriers. The key is to learn to communicate in a way that brings people closer, even when the topic is difficult or emotionally charged. In the next chapter, we will explore how to use these communication skills in conflict resolution, creating solutions that respect everyone's needs.

Chapter 9: Conflict Resolution

From Tension to Understanding: Pathways to Peace Conflicts are an inevitable part of life. What determines the health of our relationships and our inner peace is not the absence of conflict but our ability to manage and resolve them constructively. In this chapter, we will explore practical strategies for addressing and resolving conflicts that lead to greater understanding and collaboration.

Conflict: A Perspective Conflict is not inherently negative. It can serve as a signal that something needs to change or that there are unexpressed or unmet needs and desires. The key is to address it proactively and constructively.

Strategies for Conflict Resolution

1. Effective Listening: Ensure that you truly understand the other person's perspective before responding. This can help prevent misunderstandings and build trust.
2. Avoid Blame: Pointing fingers or assigning blame can make the other person defensive. Instead, focus on actions and solutions.
3. Find Common Ground: Look for areas of agreement as a basis for building a joint solution.
4. Use the "sandwich technique": Begin with positive feedback, follow with your point of concern or disagreement, and close with another positive comment.
5. Be Flexible: Sometimes, the best solution may require a compromise. Being open to

change can help find a solution that works for everyone.

6. Use the "stop and clarify" technique: If you notice the conversation is veering off track or becoming too emotional, take a break and resume when both parties are calmer.
7. Put Things in Perspective: Consider the importance of the issue in the broader context of the relationship or situation.

Exercises for Conflict Resolution

1. Hypothetical Scenarios: Consider various conflict situations and reflect on how you might respond using the strategies listed above.
2. Post-Conflict Analysis: After a disagreement or conflict, take a moment to reflect on what went well, what you could have done differently, and what you've learned.
3. Role-Playing: Practice conflict scenarios with a partner, trying different strategies to see what works best for you.

In Conclusion: Finding the Path to Peace
Remember that every relationship has its moments of tension and disagreement. What matters is how we approach these challenges and work together to build understanding and trust. With the right strategies and a genuine commitment, we can navigate anger and strengthen our relationships in the process. In the next chapter, we will explore immediate strategies for dealing with anger as it arises.

Chapter 10: Anger in Interpersonal Relationships

Navigating Turbulent Waters: Maintaining Calm in Relationships Anger, when expressed unhealthily, can seriously damage our relationships. Whether it's a family, romantic, or professional relationship, effective anger management is crucial for maintaining strong and healthy bonds. This chapter explores how to manage anger in various relational contexts and offers specific strategies for each type of relationship.

Anger in Different Relationships: An Overview • Family Relationships: Here, emotions tend to be deeper and more complex due to shared history and blood ties. • Romantic Relationships: Anger in this context can be amplified by unmet expectations and emotional vulnerability. • Professional Relationships: In these relationships, it's essential to strike a balance between healthy expression and professionalism.

Strategies for Managing Anger in Family Relationships
1. Quality Time: Regularly dedicate time to reconnect and address small issues before they become significant.
2. Establish Boundaries: Have clear discussions about what is acceptable and what is not.
3. Family Therapy: Consider seeking outside support if there are persistent issues.

Strategies for Managing Anger in Romantic Relationships

1. Open Communication: Regularly share feelings and concerns, ensuring that both parties feel heard.
2. Create Safe Spaces: Establish moments where both of you can express yourselves without fear of judgment or retaliation.
3. Couples Counseling: A valuable resource when recurring challenges arise in the relationship.

Strategies for Managing Anger in Professional Relationships

1. Pause and Reflect: Take a moment to calm down before responding to a stressful situation.
2. Constructive Feedback: If you have issues with a colleague, express your concerns constructively and solution-oriented.
3. Meditation or Relaxation Techniques: Use them to manage stress and prevent anger buildup.

Exercises for Anger Management in Relationships

1. Relational Journal: Record situations in which you felt anger in a relationship and reflect on how you handled the situation and how you could have done better.
2. Role-Playing: Simulate conflict situations with a friend or therapist and practice anger management and conflict resolution.

In Conclusion: Building Bridges, Not Barriers Remember that every relationship has its moments of tension and disagreement. What matters is how we approach these challenges and how we work together to build understanding and trust. With the right strategies and a genuine commitment, we can navigate through anger and strengthen our relationships in the process. In the next chapter, we will explore immediate strategies for dealing with anger as it arises.

Chapter 11: Immediate Control Strategies
When the Storm Arrives: Practical Guide to
Navigate Anger
Each one of us has experienced moments
when anger seems to take over. In such
moments, maintaining control can appear
impossible. However, with the right
techniques and adequate preparation, we
can confront and manage these episodes
constructively. This chapter will provide
immediate techniques to apply when anger
erupts.
Understanding Instant Anger
Immediate anger is often an instinctive
response to a perceived threat or injustice.
While it can serve as a defense mechanism,
it can also lead to impulsive and harmful
decisions.
Techniques for Immediate Control
1. Count to Ten: This classic technique gives
   your brain time to calm down and assess
   the situation before reacting.
2. Deep Breathing: By focusing on your
   breath, you can reduce your heart rate and
   calm your nervous system.

3. Time-Out: If you feel your anger is about to explode, remove yourself from the situation and give yourself time to calm down.
4. Focus: Concentrate on an object or a peaceful image, such as a picture of a loved one or a relaxing place.
5. Reframe: Ask yourself how important this situation will be in a day, a week, or a year. This can help you put things in perspective.
6. Replace Negative Thoughts: Instead of dwelling on what angered you, think of something positive or relaxing.
7. Use Positive Affirmations: Repeat phrases like "I can handle this situation" or "I am taking control of my emotions."

Tools to Keep Handy

1. Meditation App: Many smartphones have apps that offer short guided meditation sessions, useful in moments of intense stress.
2. Music: Having a playlist of relaxing or uplifting songs can be a great way to divert your attention from anger.

3. Notebook or Writing App: Writing down your feelings can help you process your anger and see it in a different light.

In Conclusion: Anger Doesn't Control You, You Do

The key to managing immediate anger is preparation. By knowing yourself and having the right techniques and tools at your disposal, you can confront and overcome even the most intense anger episodes.

Chapter 12: Recognizing Limiting Beliefs

The Invisible Chains: How Our Beliefs Shape Our Response to Anger

Each of us carries a set of beliefs acquired throughout life. These beliefs, often rooted in childhood or past experiences, can profoundly influence how we perceive and react to life events, including how we manage anger. While some of these beliefs may be helpful, others can limit us. This chapter will explore how to recognize and overcome these limiting beliefs.

The Power of Beliefs

Beliefs are like lenses through which we see the world. They can influence our behavior, emotional reactions, and even our self-esteem.

Identifying Limiting Beliefs

Some common beliefs that can influence anger management include:

1. "I don't have the right to be angry." This belief can lead to repressing anger until it explodes uncontrollably.

2. "If I show my anger, others will reject me." This can lead to avoiding conflicts at all costs, even at the expense of your own needs.

3. "Anger is a weakness." This view can prevent you from addressing and managing anger healthily.

Overcoming Limiting Beliefs

1. Reflection and Awareness: Recognizing that a belief exists is the first step in changing it.

2. Challenge Your Beliefs: Ask yourself if your belief is truly accurate and still serves you.

3. Rewrite Your Story: Replace limiting beliefs with positive affirmations that support you.
4. Therapy and Coaching: A professional can help you identify and work on deeply rooted beliefs.
5. Surround Yourself with Support: Having friends or family who encourage you can make a big difference.

Exercises to Work on Limiting Beliefs

1. Belief Journal: Write down your beliefs in a journal and assess how they influence your behavior and emotions.
2. "Challenge the Belief": Whenever you recognize a limiting belief, write a counter-argument or an example that proves it wrong.

In Conclusion: Freeing the Mind, Freeing the Soul

Limiting beliefs can act as invisible chains, holding us back and preventing us from living our best lives. Recognizing and addressing these beliefs is crucial for healthy anger management and a more fulfilling life.

Chapter 13: Forgiveness and Acceptance

The Bridge to Inner Peace: The Art of Forgiving and Accepting

Forgiveness is not only a gesture towards others but also a gift we give ourselves. Through forgiveness and acceptance, we can free ourselves from the weight of past grievances and negative feelings that hold us back, allowing us to live with greater serenity. This chapter will explore the importance of forgiveness and offer practical exercises to cultivate it in our lives.

Why Forgiveness Matters

1. Emotional Liberation: Resentment and repressed anger can become burdens. Forgiveness frees us from these emotional chains.

2. Physical Well-being: Numerous studies have shown that forgiveness can reduce stress, lower blood pressure, and improve overall health.

3. Personal Growth: Forgiveness allows us to learn from our experiences, develop empathy, and mature as individuals.

4. Reconciliation: While forgiveness does not necessarily mean reconciliation with those who hurt us, it can open the door to dialogue and understanding.

Accepting What Cannot Be Changed

Acceptance does not equal approval. It means recognizing the reality of a situation and deciding not to let it control or define our lives.

Practical Forgiveness and Acceptance Exercises

1. Forgiveness Meditation: Dedicate a few minutes each day to meditate on the concept of forgiveness. Visualize the person or situation that caused you pain and imagine releasing that burden.

2. Write a Letter: Write a letter to the person who hurt you. It is not necessary to send it, but the writing process can help you process your feelings.

3. Inner Dialogue: When you feel resentment or anger, talk to yourself. Ask why you feel that way and what you can do to release those feelings.

4. Practice Gratitude: Focus on what is positive in your life. Keeping a gratitude journal can help you concentrate on the good and let go of the negative.

5. Seek Help: If you find forgiveness difficult, consider consulting a therapist or counselor to guide you through the process.

In Conclusion: The Journey of the Heart Forgiveness and acceptance are essential steps on the path to a more peaceful and harmonious life. While it can be challenging, the benefits for our mental, physical, and emotional well-being are immense.

Chapter 14: Managing Anger in Children Small Flames, Big Eruptions: Navigating Childhood Anger

Children, with their explosive nature and lack of emotional filters, can manifest anger in ways that may seem disproportionate to adults. However, it is crucial to understand that, like adults, anger is a natural and healthy response to frustration or fear for children. This chapter will provide tools and strategies to help parents and educators manage and channel children's anger constructively.

Understanding Childhood Anger

Anger in children often has roots in feelings of powerlessness, frustration, or misunderstanding. They may not have yet developed the communication skills to express what they feel, leading to manifestations of anger.

Tools and Strategies for Parents and Educators

1. Active Listening: Listen to the child without interrupting and try to understand the source of their frustration.
2. Validation of Feelings: Even if you don't share the child's reaction, acknowledge and validate their feelings.
3. Breathing Exercises: Teach the child deep breathing techniques to help them calm down.
4. Constructive Time-Outs: Instead of punishing, use a time-out as a moment for the child to reflect and calm down.

5. Artistic Expression: Encourage the child to draw or write about what they feel. This can serve as an outlet for their emotions.
6. Role-Playing: Simulate situations that might trigger anger and work together to find solutions.
7. Set Clear Boundaries: Children thrive on structure. Providing clear rules and limits can help prevent anger episodes.
8. Role Model Behavior: Children learn by observing. Demonstrate anger management techniques in your daily routine.
9. Discuss the Future: After an anger episode has subsided, talk to the child about how they might handle a similar situation in the future.
10. Look for Early Signs: Observe the child and note any warning signs or patterns that precede an anger outburst. Intervening early can prevent a full-blown episode.

In Conclusion: Cultivating Peace from Childhood

Managing anger in children can be a challenge, but with the right tools, patience, and understanding, it is possible to help them develop emotional management skills that will serve them throughout life.

Chapter 15: Mindfulness

The Calm in the Heart of the Storm: Mindfulness and Anger Management

Mindfulness, or the practice of awareness, has its roots in ancient meditative traditions but has become increasingly popular in recent years as a therapeutic and personal growth tool. This chapter will explore how mindfulness can offer a powerful remedy for anger, helping us respond to life's challenges with balance and serenity rather than reacting impulsively.

What Is Mindfulness? Mindfulness is the ability to be fully present, aware of where we are and what we are doing, without being overly reactive or overwhelmed by what is happening around us.

Mindfulness and Anger: The Connection
1. Non-Judgmental Observation: Mindfulness teaches us to embrace our thoughts and feelings without judgment. When we experience anger, we can observe it without identifying with it or acting impulsively on it.
2. Breaking the Cycle: By practicing mindfulness, we can recognize when we are about to react with anger and choose a more considered response.
3. Identifying Triggers: Mindfulness helps us become more aware of situations, thoughts, or feelings that trigger our anger.

Mindfulness Exercises for Anger

1. Body Scan Meditation: This practice invites us to pay attention to different parts of our body, recognizing tensions and releasing them.
2. Mindful Breathing: By focusing on our breath, we can calm the mind and center ourselves, especially when we feel anger rising.
3. Walking Meditation: Walking slowly and deliberately can anchor us in the present moment and distance us from the source of our anger.
4. Recognition Exercise: When you feel anger, take a moment to recognize it: "I feel anger." This simple act of recognition can interrupt the cycle of impulsive reaction.

Mindfulness in Everyday Life
Incorporating mindfulness into your daily routine doesn't mean you have to meditate for hours every day. It can be as simple as taking a few moments to breathe deeply

during the day or taking a pause to notice how you feel physically and emotionally.

In Conclusion: Serenity Amidst the Storm Mindfulness offers a refuge of calm and awareness in the midst of life's emotional storms. Through regular practice, we can develop an anger management capacity rooted in kindness towards ourselves and others. In the next chapter, we will explore when and how to seek professional support for anger management.
Chapter 16: Therapy and Professional Support

A Bridge to Balance: Seeking Professional Help in Anger Management While many people find relief and effective strategies through individual practice and personal growth, there are times when anger becomes too overwhelming or damaging. In such situations, seeking professional help can be the key to restoring balance and finding lasting solutions.

When to Seek Professional Help?

1. Uncontrollable Anger: When anger becomes too intense or frequent and negatively impacts your daily life.
2. Harming Yourself or Others: When anger leads to violent or self-destructive behaviors.
3. Relationship Issues: If anger is causing problems in your personal or professional relationships.
4. Legal Involvement: Situations where anger has led to legal issues, such as assaults or property damage.

The Benefits of Therapy

1. Safe Environment: A therapist provides a neutral and confidential environment to express and explore your anger.
2. Deep Understanding: With the help of a professional, you can delve deeper into the underlying causes of your anger.
3. Tools and Strategies: Therapists can provide specific tools and techniques for managing and channeling anger in healthy ways.

4. Ongoing Support: Therapy offers regular support, helping you stay on the right track in your anger management journey.

Types of Therapies for Anger

1. Cognitive-Behavioral Therapy (CBT): This approach focuses on recognizing and changing negative thoughts and behaviors.
2. Interpersonal Therapy: It concentrates on improving communication skills and resolving issues in relationships.
3. Support Groups: Groups of people facing similar challenges can offer understanding, advice, and mutual support.
4. Mind-Body Therapies: Approaches like biofeedback or meditation that connect the mind and body to manage emotional reactions.

How to Find the Right Therapist

1. Ask for Referrals: Doctors, friends, or colleagues may have recommendations.
2. Initial Assessment: Many therapists offer initial sessions to determine if they are a good fit for your needs.

3. Experience and Specialization: Seek a professional with expertise in anger management or related issues.
4. Trust Your Instinct: It's important to feel comfortable and confident in the therapist you choose.

In Conclusion: External Help as a Bridge to Harmony While self-management and personal strategies are essential, sometimes we need an external anchor to help us navigate emotional storms. Therapy and professional support can be that compass guiding us to calmer waters. In the next chapter, we will discuss preventive strategies to avoid anger flare-ups.
Chapter 17: Anger Prevention

Anticipation as the Key: Reducing the Frequency and Intensity of Anger If anger management is the first step in maintaining emotional balance, prevention is the wise strategy to minimize the circumstances where this management becomes necessary. Through understanding and applying preventive strategies, we can reduce the frequency and intensity of anger episodes in our lives.

Preventive Strategies: The Foundation

1. Self-Knowledge: Understanding your triggers or provoking causes is essential. Recognizing the situations or people who tend to provoke you can help you avoid or prepare for such situations.
2. Stress Management: Stress is a major cause of anger. Find relaxation techniques like meditation or yoga to help you manage daily stress.
3. Maintain a Life Balance: Ensure you have time for yourself, activities you love, and rest. A well-rested body and mind are less prone to anger reactions.
4. Positive Expression: Find healthy ways to express your emotions, such as writing, drawing, or talking to a trusted friend.
5. Cognitive Training: Learn to recognize and challenge negative or distorted thoughts that can fuel anger.

Creating a Positive Environment
1. Surround Yourself with Positivity:
   Surround yourself with people and
   situations that uplift your spirits and give
   you a positive perspective on life.
2. Set Boundaries: Learn to say "no" and
   establish limits that help you avoid
   stressful or conflict-ridden situations.
3. Avoid Isolation: Share your concerns or
   frustrations with others. Sometimes,
   talking about them can relieve tension and
   prevent the buildup of anger.

Nutrition and Physical Health
1. Balanced Diet: Eating healthy and
   balanced foods can influence your mood
   and your ability to manage stress.
2. Physical Exercise: Physical activity helps
   release tension and produces endorphins,
   natural chemicals that promote happiness.
3. Avoid Stimulants and Depressants:
   Alcohol, caffeine, and certain drugs can
   alter your mood and your ability to manage
   anger.

In Conclusion: Prevention as a Lifestyle
Preventing anger doesn't mean eliminating all potential sources of frustration from your life. Instead, it means developing a mindset and habits that allow you to approach life with a more balanced and peaceful perspective. In the next chapter, we will delve into the stories of those who have transformed their anger into something positive.

Chapter 18: Success Stories

The Power of Transformation Uncontrolled anger can cause significant damage in our lives and relationships with others. However, with the right approach and suitable strategies, it's possible to transform it into a powerful catalyst for personal change and growth. In this chapter, we will share some inspirational testimonies of individuals who have managed to turn their anger into something constructive and positive.

1. Marco: From Boxer to Mediator Marco was known for his explosive nature. Once, during an argument with a colleague, he threw a punch that cost him his job and a lawsuit. Instead of sinking deeper into anger, Marco decided to seek help. Thanks to therapy and meditation techniques, he not only learned to control his anger but also used his conflict resolution skills to become a professional mediator.

2. Giulia: Turning Anger into Art After a painful breakup, Giulia found herself overwhelmed by anger and frustration. Instead of letting these feelings consume her, she decided to channel them into painting. Over time, her canvases became expressions of her emotions, transforming her anger into beautiful artworks that touched the hearts of those who viewed them.

3. Andrea: The Successful Athlete Andrea grew up in a tough neighborhood where anger and violence were the norm. For him, the solution was basketball. Instead of venting his anger on the streets, Andrea dedicated himself entirely to the sport. Every time he felt anger rising, he channeled it onto the court. This determination led him to earn a scholarship to university and later become a professional player.

4. Elisa: Anger as Motivation After being unjustly fired, Elisa felt angry and betrayed. Instead of letting it get her down, she used that anger as fuel to start her own business. She now runs one of the largest companies in her industry, providing employment to many people and demonstrating that with the right mindset, anger can be a powerful driver of success.

In Conclusion: Anger as an Opportunity
The stories of Marco, Giulia, Andrea, and Elisa are just a few among the many testimonies of those who have managed to transform anger from an enemy into an ally. Each story is unique, but they all share a fundamental lesson: with determination, support, and the right strategies, anger can become an opportunity to grow and achieve unexpected success. In the next chapter, we will provide practical exercises to help you put into practice what you've learned.
Chapter 19: Practical Exercises

Putting Theory into Action Understanding anger and its dynamics is essential, but putting into practice what we've learned is the real step towards transformation. In this chapter, we will provide a series of practical exercises to help you manage, express, and transform your anger constructively.

1. Anger Journal Objective: Increase awareness of situations that trigger anger.
   - Take a notebook and jot down every time you feel angry.
   - Write down the situation, the time of day, what triggered your anger, and how you felt.
   - After a week, review your notes. Look for patterns or recurring themes.

---

2. Square Breathing Objective: Calm the nervous system and reduce immediate anger.
   - Find a quiet place.
   - Breathe slowly, counting to 4.
   - Hold your breath for a count of 4.
   - Exhale slowly, counting to 4.
   - Repeat for at least 5 minutes.

---

3. Story Rewrite Objective: Change your perspective on past events that cause anger.
    - Think of a past event that still makes you angry.
    - Write the story as you remember it.
    - Now, try to rewrite it from a different perspective or imagine a positive outcome.

4. Dialogue with Anger Objective: Gain better understanding of the origins of your anger.
    - Imagine your anger as a person sitting in front of you.
    - Ask your anger questions. Ask why it's present and what it wants.
    - Listen to the answers. You may discover valuable insights into your hidden emotions.

5. Feedback Training Objective: Express feelings of anger constructively.
    - With a friend or family member, practice sharing feedback using the

formula "When you... I feel... because...".

- This method allows you to express anger without blaming the other person.

---

6. Empathy Meditation Objective: Develop empathy and reduce anger toward others.
    - Sit comfortably and close your eyes.
    - Think of a person who recently made you angry.
    - Imagine seeing the world through their eyes, including their stresses and challenges.
    - Open your heart to understanding and empathy.

Conclusion: Practice makes perfect. Continue to work with these activities, adapting them to your needs. Over time, you'll notice a decrease in anger episodes and an increased ability to handle situations constructively. In the next chapter, we will discuss how to design a continuous growth path towards a life without anger.
Chapter 20: The Path to a Life Without Anger

Continuous Transformation Managing anger is not a one-time achievement. Instead, it's an ongoing journey of growth and learning. However, with the right tools and a clear vision, you can build a life where anger doesn't dominate your reactions but serves as a signal for greater self-understanding.

1. Vision and Values Objective: Define a clear vision of the life you want, where anger is managed healthily.
    - Write a vision statement for yourself, envisioning your life without the constant shadow of anger.
    - List the core values you want to honor in your life, such as respect, patience, or understanding.

2. Proactive Planning Objective: Anticipate and prevent situations that might trigger anger.
    - Take note of situations that, as you've learned, tend to trigger your anger.
    - Think of proactive ways to handle these situations in the future, like avoiding specific triggers or preparing calm responses in advance.

3. Support Network Objective: Surround yourself with people who support you in your anger management journey.

- Identify friends, family, or professionals who can assist you when you feel overwhelmed.
- Establish a "check-in" system with these individuals where they can provide feedback or simply listen.

4. Review and Reflection Objective: Regularly assess your progress and adjust your anger management plan accordingly.
   - Dedicate time every week or month to reflect on your progress.
   - Review your "Anger Journal" and note any improvements or areas that require further attention.

5. Ongoing Education Objective: Stay updated on the latest research and anger management techniques.
   - Attend seminars, read books, or join support groups dedicated to anger management.
   - Share what you learn with others, contributing to a community of people managing anger healthily.

6. Celebrate Your Successes Objective: Recognize and celebrate your progress along the way.

- When you notice improvements in how you manage anger, take a moment to acknowledge it.
- Treat yourself to small rewards, like a relaxing day or a special treat.

Conclusion: Remember, the path to a life without anger is a journey, not a destination. There will be ups and downs, but with commitment, awareness, and the right strategies, you can build a life characterized by inner peace, healthy relationships, and self-fulfillment. Keep walking with determination and compassion towards yourself.
Conclusion

Anger is a universal emotion, a natural human response to threats, frustrations, or injustices. But, as we've explored throughout this book, the key is not to suppress or deny this emotion but rather to understand, embrace, and manage anger constructively.

Anger management is not just about avoiding conflicts or maintaining peace. It goes much deeper. It's about living a more authentic, mindful, and fulfilling life. When we learn how to manage anger, we give ourselves the opportunity to respond to life's challenges not with impulsive reactivity but with awareness and intentionality. In this way, we can make wiser decisions, build stronger relationships, and live with a sense of inner peace.

The journey towards effective anger management is not always easy. There may be times when we feel overwhelmed, frustrated, or discouraged. But, as we've seen, with the right strategies, resources, and support, we can transform our anger from an enemy into an ally, from a shadow that darkens our life into a light that illuminates our path towards greater self-understanding and personal growth.

In conclusion, I want to encourage every reader to continue on their journey of exploring and managing anger. Whether you're just starting or well underway in this journey, know that every step, no matter how small, brings you closer to a more peaceful, balanced, and harmonious version of yourself.

Remember that emotional well-being is not a destination but a journey. And as you embark on this journey, be kind to yourself, acknowledge your progress, and celebrate every success along the way.

Your ability to manage anger is a gift not only to yourself but also to the people around you, to your relationships, and to the world at large. Keep nurturing and cultivating this ability, and you'll see how it can transform your life in ways you might never have imagined.

Thank you for sharing this path of learning and growth. I wish you every success in your ongoing journey towards emotional well-being.

Appendix • Additional resources, books, courses, and references on the topic.

Appendix

Additional Resources and Recommended Readings Understanding and managing anger are vast and evolving fields of study. If you wish to delve further, here are some recommended resources that can provide you with additional information and tools:

1. Books:
   - "The Dance of Anger" by Harriet Lerner - A deep analysis of anger in women and how to transform it into a positive force.

- "The Art of Mindful Living" by Thich Nhat Hanh - A Buddhist interpretation of anger management through mindfulness and meditation.
- "Anger: Handling a Powerful Emotion" by Gary Chapman - Explores the roots of anger and offers practical techniques for managing it.

2. Online Courses:
- "Anger Management 101" - An introductory course providing a comprehensive overview of anger's causes, effects, and management techniques.
- "Mindfulness and Anger" - A course that combines mindfulness practices with anger management techniques.

3. Organizations and Support Groups:
- Anger & Stress Management Centre (www.angerstress.com) - Offers resources, training, and support for individuals and professionals.
- Anger Management Support Groups - Local groups that provide meetings

and sessions for sharing experiences and strategies on anger management.

4. Scientific References and Articles:
   - Journal of Anger and Aggression - An academic journal dedicated to research on anger and aggression.
   - "Anger and the Brain" - An article exploring the neurological and biological aspects of anger.

5. Apps and Digital Tools:
   - Calm - A meditation and relaxation app with specific sessions for managing strong emotions like anger.
   - Mood Tracker - An app that helps you monitor and understand your daily emotions, including anger. Remember, the key is to find what works best for you. Not all tools or resources will be suitable for everyone, so take the time to explore and discover what resonates with you the most. Your commitment to understanding and managing your anger is a valuable investment in your well-being and that of the people

around you. Safe travels on your journey!

Conclusion: A Journey Toward Understanding and Managing Anger

You have embarked on a profound and comprehensive journey through understanding anger, its origins, its manifestations, and, most importantly, strategies for managing it and transforming it into a constructive rather than destructive force. Anger, as you've seen, is not necessarily an emotion to avoid or suppress but rather to understand, accept, and channel in productive ways. Summary of key points:

1. Definition and understanding of anger: Anger is a natural reaction to certain situations, linked to our biological and psychological mechanisms.

2. Anger management: Important for our mental and physical health.

3. Recognizing signs: Awareness of physical and emotional signals can help prevent anger outbursts.

4. Origins and types of anger: Understanding the causes and different manifestations of anger helps us manage it better.

5. Tools and strategies: From mindfulness to therapy, there are many effective strategies for managing anger.

Additional resources to explore: To continue your journey of growth and understanding of anger, I recommend visiting the following websites and guides:

1. Anger Management Institute (www.angermanagementinstitute.com): A comprehensive resource for courses, training, and information on anger management.

2. Mindful.org (www.mindful.org): Offers articles and guides on mindfulness, which can be a valuable tool in managing strong emotions like anger.

3. Italian Association for Anger Management (AIGR) (www.aigr.org): A specific resource for Italians, with articles, research, and courses on the topic. If you feel that your anger is negatively impacting your life or relationships, consider seeking help from a

professional. Therapists and counselors can provide personalized tools, resources, and support to assist you. Ultimately, your commitment to managing anger can lead you to a more peaceful, happier life that is in harmony with yourself and others. Your willingness to address and work with your anger is a sign of strength and wisdom. Keep on your path and find peace and clarity in your emotional responses.
Safe travels toward a deeper understanding and effective management of your anger!

Chapter 21: Anger Across Cultures

While anger is a universal emotion, it is influenced and shaped by numerous cultural, social, and historical factors. The way it manifests, is expressed, and managed can vary significantly from one culture to another. These differences can stem from a myriad of factors, including religious beliefs, social norms, history, and traditions.

How different cultures and societies perceive and manage anger: The perception and management of anger are closely tied to the cultural values and norms of a society. For example, in some Asian cultures like Japanese and Chinese, anger is often seen as a manifestation of losing control and can be stigmatized. Open expression of anger may be considered socially unacceptable, leading people to repress or mask their anger.

Conversely, in some Western cultures, expressing one's anger assertively (but not aggressively) can be seen as a sign of honesty and authenticity. However, even in these cultures, there are social guidelines on when and how it is appropriate to manifest anger.

Historical and contemporary examples of anger management from around the world:
• Ancient Greece: Anger, known as "thumos" in ancient Greek, was often associated with the desire for vengeance. It was both praised as a driver of courage in battle and criticized when it led to unnecessary conflicts. Mythological figures like Achilles are examples of how anger could be both a source of strength and weakness.
• India: The concept of "Krodh" in Sikhism is one of the five vices or passions that an individual must control. In Buddhism, anger is seen as one of the three roots of evil, along with desire and ignorance.

• Indigenous cultures: Many indigenous peoples around the world have specific rituals and ceremonies for managing and transforming anger and other negative emotions, recognizing their power but also their potential for destruction.

• Modern societies: With the advent of social media and digital communications, anger has found new ways to manifest itself, often amplified and distorted. However, many cultures are also recognizing the importance of anger management and emotional education, leading to greater awareness and understanding of this powerful emotion.

In conclusion, while anger in its essence may be universal, its context, expression, and management are deeply rooted in the cultural fabric of each society. Understanding these differences can offer valuable insights into how to effectively and constructively manage anger in a globalized society.

Chapter 22: Neurobiology of Anger

Anger, like all emotions, has deep roots in our brain. More precisely, it can be localized and studied through the network of neural structures and connections that collaborate to produce, regulate, and manifest this powerful emotion. Having a better understanding of what happens in our brain when anger occurs can equip us to manage it effectively.

What happens in the brain when we get angry: When a situation or stimulus is perceived as a threat or a source of frustration, our brain initiates a complex processing sequence. This begins with the perception of the stimulus through our senses, which is then processed by various brain structures to determine an appropriate response. If the response is anger, a series of neurobiological events are set in motion:

- Amygdala: This small almond-shaped structure in our brain plays a crucial role in perceiving and reacting to threats. It is essentially the brain's alarm system. When we perceive a stimulus as threatening, the amygdala activates, leading to a rapid emotional response, such as anger. The amygdala acts very quickly, often before we are consciously aware of the threat, preparing us to react.

- Prefrontal Cortex: Located in the front part of the brain, the prefrontal cortex is involved in higher functions such as decision-making, planning, inhibiting impulsive responses, and regulating emotions. When it comes to anger, the prefrontal cortex can moderate or inhibit the automatic responses generated by the amygdala. For example, it might tell us to pause and reflect before reacting impulsively in an anger-inducing situation. The interplay between the amygdala and prefrontal cortex is fundamental in anger management. When they function optimally, the prefrontal cortex helps us regulate and control our immediate responses generated by the amygdala. However, if there is excessive activity in

the amygdala or inadequate regulation by the prefrontal cortex, we may encounter difficulties in managing our anger.
In conclusion, anger is a complex phenomenon involving multiple brain structures and functions. A better understanding of its neurobiology can provide us with valuable tools to manage this emotion more consciously and effectively.

Chapter 23: Anger and Gender

Gender plays a significant role in our society and influences how people experience and interpret emotions, including anger. There are entrenched cultural and social perceptions that portray men as more aggressive and women as more emotional. But do these generalizations hold up under scientific scrutiny? Let's explore gender differences in the expression and management of anger and what recent studies have to say on the subject.

Differences in the expression and management of anger between men and women:

- Men: Traditionally, in most cultures, men have been taught to suppress their emotions, except for anger, which is often seen as a socially acceptable emotion for them. Men may express anger in more direct ways, such as physical or verbal aggression. Additionally, they may be less likely to talk about their feelings or seek alternative solutions when they are angry.
- Women: On the other hand, women are often encouraged to express their emotions, but at the same time, they may feel discouraged from showing anger due to social perceptions that label female anger as "hysterical" or "irrational." As a result, women may express anger indirectly, through withdrawal or silence, or they may express it as sadness or frustration rather than pure anger. Studies and research on the correlation between anger and gender:

- Some studies suggest that differences in the expression of anger between men and women may be more a matter of socialization than biology. This means that from a young age, we are taught, through examples and feedback, how we should behave based on our gender.
- Recently, with the evolution of discussions on gender fluidity and the acceptance of non-binary identities, research has expanded to explore how individuals outside the traditional gender binary experience and manage anger.
- It is interesting to note that culture and socialization play a significant role in shaping our perception of gender-related anger. In some cultures, for example, women may be just as explicitly aggressive as men without stigma.

In conclusion, while biological differences between genders may have some impact on emotions and behavior, culture, socialization, and gender expectations have a predominant role in determining how men, women, and non-binary individuals express and manage anger. It is essential to move beyond gender stereotypes and understand anger as a universal human emotion influenced by a myriad of internal and external factors.

Chapter 24: Anger in the Digital World

With the expansion of digital technologies and the omnipresence of social media, anger has found new channels of expression. The online world, while offering countless opportunities for connection and communication, has also presented unique challenges in the expression and management of anger. This chapter will explore how anger manifests in the digital world and provide tools and techniques for effectively managing it. How anger manifests in the online world:

- Social media discussions: The often impersonal nature of online interactions can make people feel free to express anger in ways they might not do in person. This can lead to heated discussions where the escalation of anger becomes rapid and uncontrollable.

- Toxic comments and trolls: The phenomenon of "trolls" on the internet involves individuals deliberately provoking others to elicit a reaction. Their motivation often stems from a desire to garner attention and create conflicts.
- Cyberbullying: This form of online bullying can have devastating impacts on the mental and emotional well-being of victims. Aggressors often use anger and aggression as tools to intimidate and torment others online.

Tools and techniques for managing anger online:

- Pause before responding: Taking a moment to breathe and reflect before responding to an irritating comment or post can help prevent the escalation of emotions.
- Limit exposure: If certain topics, groups, or individuals tend to trigger anger, it may be helpful to limit exposure to such triggers.

- Use of filters and parental controls: These tools can help filter out offensive or inappropriate content, reducing opportunities for confrontation.
- Digital literacy education: Courses and programs that teach young people and adults how to behave online, emphasizing the importance of digital courtesy and emotional management in the virtual world.
- Seeking support: Online groups and forums that offer support and advice on how to manage anger and online aggression can be valuable resources.

In conclusion, while the digital realm has made it easier than ever to connect with others, it has also brought new challenges in anger management. Having tools and strategies to navigate the online world in a healthy and respectful manner, preventing the escalation of conflicts, and promoting understanding is essential.

Chapter 25: Anger and Creativity

Anger, although often perceived as a destructive emotion, can also become a powerful catalyst for creativity. Many artists, writers, and creators have discovered that anger, when channeled productively, can lead to profound, thought-provoking, and revolutionary works of art. This chapter explores how anger can be transformed into creative expression and provides testimonials from artists who have used this powerful emotion as a source of inspiration.

How to channel anger into forms of art and creative expression:

- Writing: Anger can be transformed into words, poetry, stories, or essays. Writing allows one to explore and process the emotion, turning it into meaningful narrative.
- Visual arts: Painting, sculpture, photography, and other forms of visual art can become a means to represent and process feelings of anger. The use of color, shape, and texture can express intensity and passions.

- Music: Many musicians have used anger as a starting point to create powerful songs or compositions. Genres like punk, rock, and rap, in particular, have often tackled themes of anger and resistance.
- Dance: Body movement can become a means to express and release anger. Dance allows the channeling of energy physically, transforming the emotion into action. Testimonials from artists who have used anger as inspiration:
- Frida Kahlo: Through her works, Kahlo often explored themes of pain, suffering, and anger stemming from her personal experiences of physical and emotional trauma.
- The Clash: This punk band is known for their anger-filled songs that address themes of social and political injustice.
- Maya Angelou: In her works, Angelou confronted themes of anger, racism, and discrimination, using her voice to explore and condemn injustices.

- Ai Weiwei: This Chinese artist and activist used his art as a means to express his anger against government oppression and censorship in China.

In summary, while anger can be a destructive force, when channeled creatively, it can also become a source of inspiration, resistance, and change. The ability to transform anger into art is a powerful means of expression and healing.

Chapter 26: Anger and Sports

Sports have always represented an outlet, a release, and a source of discipline for many individuals. The very nature of sports, combining physical exertion with mental strategy, makes it a particularly useful activity for those seeking to manage intense emotions like anger. This chapter examines how sports can become an effective tool in anger management and the benefits that physical activity can bring to emotional regulation.

Using sports as an outlet and anger management:

- Physical expression: Anger often manifests through accumulated physical energy. Sports, with their physical movements and efforts, provide an opportunity to release this energy in a controlled and structured environment.
- Focus and discipline: Many sports disciplines require a high level of concentration. This focus can help divert

attention from anger triggers and channel it toward a sporting goal.

- Learning to lose: Sports teach that losing is part of the game. This lesson can help develop greater resilience and better frustration management, often at the core of anger.

Benefits of physical activity in emotion regulation:

- Release of endorphins: Physical activity stimulates the body to produce endorphins, also known as "feel-good hormones." These natural chemicals act as analgesics and improve mood, helping to neutralize feelings of anger.
- Stress reduction: Physical exercise is known to reduce stress levels, a primary cause of anger. Sports help alleviate muscle tension and promote a sense of well-being.
- Enhanced self-esteem: Participation in sports can strengthen self-confidence and self-esteem, reducing feelings of vulnerability that can trigger anger.
- Social development: Team sports, in particular, offer an opportunity to interact

with others, learning to work together and manage conflicts constructively.

In conclusion, sports represent a powerful tool for those seeking to manage and transform their anger. The combination of physical effort, mental discipline, and social interaction makes sports a valuable ally in handling intense emotions.

Chapter 27: The Relationship Between Anger and Other Emotions

Anger is often like the tip of an iceberg: what we see on the surface represents only a small part of what lies beneath the surface. Many times, this powerful emotion can mask or be closely connected to other emotions. Understanding and recognizing these connections can offer a key to effectively managing anger. In this chapter, we will explore the relationship between anger and other emotions and provide techniques for investigating underlying emotions.

How anger can mask or be connected to other emotions:

- Anger and Sadness: It is not uncommon for anger to mask deep sadness or disappointment. For example, an individual may express anger after a romantic breakup, but beneath that anger, there may be a profound sense of loss or grief.

- Anger and Fear: Anger can be a defensive response to dangerous or threatening situations. In this context, anger acts as armor, protecting the individual from the vulnerability of fear.
- Anger and Anxiety: Anxiety, with its incessant worries, can lead to feelings of frustration and helplessness, which, in turn, can trigger anger.
Techniques to defuse anger by exploring underlying emotions:
- Introspection: Take a moment to reflect inwardly and ask yourself, "What am I really feeling? Is my anger masking another emotion?"
- Mindfulness techniques: The practice of mindfulness can help recognize and separate anger from underlying emotions, allowing you to address each emotion distinctly.
- Assertive communication: Expressing your feelings clearly and non-aggressively can help clarify the causes of anger and address them more productively.

- Therapy and counseling: A therapist can help explore the underlying emotions beneath anger and provide tools for managing them.

In conclusion, recognizing that anger can be tied to or masked by other emotions is crucial for effective management. Working to understand and address these underlying emotions can lead to greater inner peace and emotional balance.

Conclusion of the Section:

Through these final chapters, we have explored additional facets and dimensions of anger. From its relationship with culture and neurobiology to its manifestations in the digital age, its connection to creativity, sports, and other emotions, it is clear that anger is a complex emotion, deeply rooted in our experiences and influenced by a multitude of factors.

The key to effective anger management does not lie in suppressing or ignoring this emotion but in accepting it, understanding it, and using appropriate tools and techniques to channel it constructively. Resources for Further Exploration: For those wishing to delve further into the topic, we recommend consulting the following websites and guides:

1. Italian Association of Psychology
2. Center for Mindfulness and Cognitive Therapy
3. Support Network for Anger Management

Furthermore, numerous courses, seminars, and workshops are available in many cities, offering practical training and support in anger management.

Thank you for embarking on this journey with us. May you find inner peace and the answers you seek in your path of understanding and managing anger.

Conclusion of the Book:

As we come to the end of this journey, let us reflect on a fundamental concept: anger, like all emotions, is part of the human condition. It is neither good nor bad in itself; what matters is how we choose to respond to it.

Everything we have discussed and learned in this book provides the foundation for addressing anger consciously and constructively. If there is one thing to remember, it is that the path to effective anger management is an ongoing journey of learning, introspection, and personal growth.

9 798886 904341 2